Author, Audrey Clausen

Co-Authored by Nina Boyd and Steve Severance

ISBN: 1517430917
ISBN-13: 9781517430917

DEDICATION

This book is dedicated to all those who stand for "no tolerance" regarding racial bigotry.

Thank you to partners Nina Boyd anI would like to dedicate this book d Steve Severance for your steady passion and vigilance having the same goals as I do to Start the Conversation on Race Equality Yourself.

Author, Audrey Clausen

I would like to thank my loving husband Dale and my wonderful daughters Tiffany, Brittany and Stephanie for always encouraging me to contribute to making the world a better place.
Blessings to all.

Co-author, Nina Boyd

I would like to thank my husband, Tim Nelson, my children Julian and Annika, my parents, John and Ann Rolloff and my friends for encouraging me to continue my work for social justice and for starting a conversation on racial equality.

Co-author, Stephen Severance

I would like to thank the experiences of working with students and parents and the leadership of Yusef Mgeni for enduring me to carry out my passion for social justice and youth programming.

Changing minds,
Changing lives.

"Burrrrr, Burrrrr," today is kind of a chilly day! Autumn can be such an unpredictable season.   Some days it may feel just like summer is back and smiles on us for a day or two. But Autumn leaves on the trees are turning a beautiful brilliant orange, yellow, red and brown!

Scorey thinks about what happened this past summer with a sad feeling inside.

He says to himself "I am glad for autumn because that is when school starts. Will all the craziness about our colors stop?

"Scorey" the Cockatoo

In September we all come to school together, just different colors, shapes and sizes.

"Leonard, aka Lenny " the Blue Parrot Bird

"Clara" the African Grey Parrot

"Petie" the Yellow Parrot

Jazzy the Green Macaw Parrot

We all live in the same kinds of dwellings.

There are so many confusing things happening! Some of the birds in the trees think that because of their colors, they are the smartest, wisest, and prettiest of all the parrots in the trees!

Some parrots want my family to move out of the trees! I overheard Petie, the Green Macaw parrot, whispering to my friend Jazzy, another Green Macaw parrot, "Why do they have to live in the same tree as us? They can move to their own tree!"

Suddenly all the parrots in the trees are loudly squawking the same message.

Scorey asks, "Jazzy, so what is the big fight about? We all have wings to fly. We should be able to live in any tree we want to!"

Jazzy replies, "Well, no we can't according those squawkers over there! Oh, I mean other parrots."

Jazzy doesn't know what to say and can tell that Scorey is feeling uncomfortable.

Scorey sits on the edge of the branch feeling a little lost. Mom, is making dinner and notices Scorey. She asks "My son, you are looking kind of gloomy over there, what's up little one?"

Scorey says, "Mom, please don't call me little one anymore! I am a big one and I can handle anything!"

"Well, what got you in this kind of mood?" asks mom as she turns her back to pick food for dinner.

Scorey begins to explain to mom what he overheard Petie whispering to Jazzy. Scorey begins to repeat word by word what he clearly heard!

Mom seems to be mulling it over in her head with a little smile. Yet, when dad comes home she expresses her concerns about what to do or say to Scorey.

Scorey hears dad say, "Well, I hope this doesn't get out of hand!"

Mom shrugs her beak up in the air and says, "Hummmm, I smell trouble in the air."

Dad answers, "Mother, please don't worry! We have very good parrots surrounding us. Plus, we always have "Old Sergeant McGulleny" if anyone gets out of hand!"

Mom turns back to me and says "Scorey, just don't make a big deal out of this to anyone. This too shall pass!"

"Okay, Okay," I think. But as the days go on, the squawking parrots get louder and louder and meaner and meaner demanding that we move out!

Scorey feels so uncomfortable living in this grove of community trees!

All the families are perched in the trees with their beaks raised high to the sky, squawking loudly.

"Move out! Move out! You are not the same color as we are, we are beautiful with different colors and you are not! You are just plain blue and white."

The evening is getting cold and dark. Scorey's community spends the evenings in the tree.

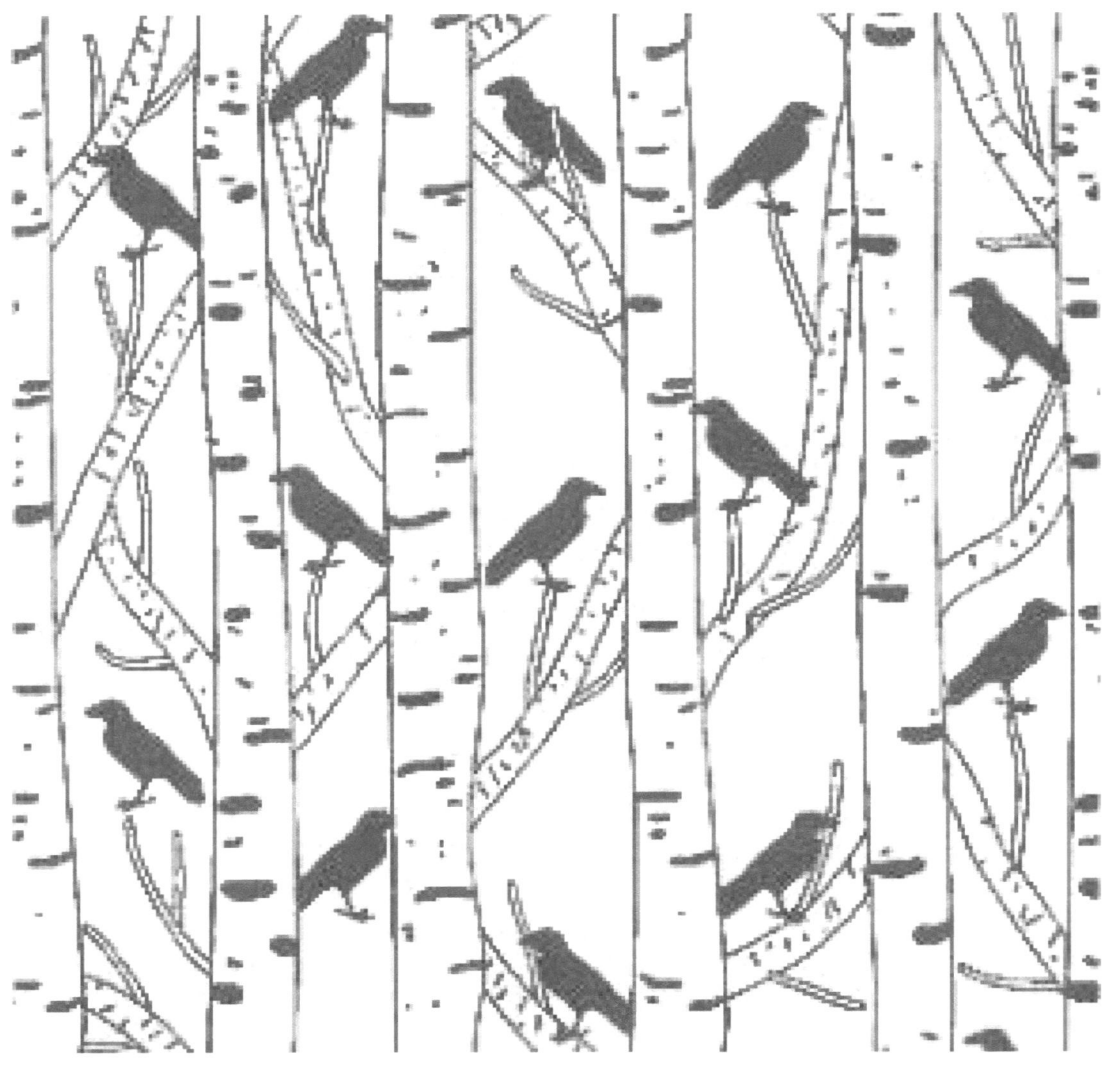

Scorey starts to cry. He shouts back with all the strength he can muster, "I am just as beautiful as you because it isn't the feathers

on the outside but the goodness you share from the inside that matters."

They chant back, "Ring around the collar, you fall down!" as the Macaw pushes Scorey out of the tree to the ground.

Momma Parrot patches me up, but I will forever remember this day when I got the ugly scar.

Scorey's parents see what is happening. Daddy Parrot flies after the Macaw to find his parents to tell them what happened. Mom Parrot flies to the ground and picks up Scorey to fly back to their home.

After Daddy Parrot talks with the parents of the Macaw he returns home frustrated and disappointed.

Mom asks, "My dear, why are you looking so concerned?"

"Dearest Mother, I am afraid that Scorey is right. Maybe we should move from this neighborhood tree and find another one to call our home. These parrots care more about what color we are than the fact that we are good neighbors!"

Mother says, "But dearest Papa, I just got our nest the way I like it! Isn't there something we can do to keep our home here? And what if the new community turns out to be the same as this one?"

Scorey says, "I have an idea! We can get our friends and family that live in surrounding communities to rally for everyone to live together and let everyone accept each other."

"Parrot Lives Matter!"

Big parrots, small parrots, and lots of other parrots come from the North, South, East and West. Scorey thinks, "I didn't know that many parrots care!" Scorey has a friendly smile on his face when he sees them and realizes what they are getting ready to do!

The community is so moved by the movement that they decide to work with Scorey and his family. They help them clean and restore their nest. Learning to work together makes everyone appreciate each other, realizing that "Parrot Lives Matter!"

This book was inspired by S.C.O.R.E. game.

Start A Conversation on Race Equality for more information go to WWW.racismisbullying.com

People playing S.C.O.R.E.

Author biography

Audrey Clausen created a
diversity/inclusion game S.C.O.R.E.

which stands for Start a Conversation On Race Equality. She formerly worked with Washington County, District 833 in Minnesota as an educational staff member. She's had twenty years of experience with grades levels from elementary to secondary. As an African American woman, she became proactive instead of reactive when it came to hearing derogatory comments from students and staff. The comments made were intentionally and unintentionally, offensive. She discovered ways to teach us how to get along and learn to discover our differences and embrace them.

www.ingramcontent.com/pod-product-compliance
Lightning Source LLC
Chambersburg PA
CBHW060815290526
45792CB00005BB/1665